MW01711661

CONNECT W

FOR HEALING AND WELLNESS WITH HYPNOSIS

21 DAYS TO BODY MIND & SOUL HEALING

A simple Technique To Change Your Life For The Better

ALEX SZWED CCHt.

Copyright © 2021 by Alex Szwed

All rights reserved. Without limiting the rights under copyright reserved above, no part of this book may be reproduced, stored, or introduced into a retrieval system, or transmitted, in any form or by any means (electronically, mechanical, photocopying, or recording or otherwise), with the prior written permission of copywrite owner and the publisher.

ISBN: 9798702593289

DISCLAMER

Since the success or failure of any therapy depends upon many unknown factors, it is almost Impossible to ascertain (within a reasonable degree of certainty) what response any individual may exhibit during the hypnotic session. Hypnotherapy is not a medical procedure, nor is it the practice of medicine. No hypnotherapist should guarantee the anticipated response or result of a hypnotic session.

CONTENTS

Part 1

Part 2

Part 3

Part 4

Part 5

PART 1

WHO SHOULD READ THIS BOOK?

In this book, I will try to touch on different aspects of understanding hypnosis, and how it is being utilized for various problems in one life or how it can benefit and improve one's life with the power of the mind.

Join me as I discuss some of the major points of view regarding the power of the mind and how hypnosis can heal you.

Every year I work with hundreds of people and educate them about the value of hypnosis and the power of their mind. My objective is to reveal to you how you can take control of your life and achieve your dreams and goals with remarkable ease. This book can guide you to higher personal and professional satisfaction.

I know these are strong claims, but over the years I have seen the proof. I would hesitate to even suggest such benefits, however the data is irrefutable.

Thanks to popular culture, hypnotism has achieved an eerie, mystical, otherworldly, and sometimes evil reputation. Yes, hypnosis is powerful by verbal suggestion. People under hypnosis can be made to do and believe things and therefore act as a different person. There is certainly a lot more than meets the eye about hypnotism.

As one of the most intriguing, yet also one of the most bewildering topics to come across time, hypnotism transcends boundaries as it continues to be studied, analyzed, and interpreted in diverse fields of wisdom. From medicine, psychology, new age, self-help, religion, history, media, and popular culture, hypnotism is bestowed with different meanings, interpretations, and uses. The conclusions are never final, and the reports are ever evolving.

This may be rooted from one thesis: Hypnotism is an exploration of the human mind; evolving, infinitely powerful.

Explore or reject the possibility of programming the human mind and the life of the person is an idea to be reckoned with. But please should you decide to move further into the topic – be aware that nobody is controlling your decision, and anything you engage in shall be done of your own free will!

Your subconscious mind is a tool that controls who you are, and what you are. This tool does not take a lot of time, nor is it expensive. It only requires a small investment of your time and willingness to experience its myriad of applications. It is that Simple.

Allow yourself to venture down the path to wellness, and happiness.

I know these are strong claims, but over the years, I have seen the proof. I would hesitate to even suggest such benefits, but after hundreds of clients that have experienced hypnosis with me, and have had success in their sessions, the data is irrefutable.

MY PROMISE TO YOU

As the title of the book states, 21 Days to Body, Mind and Soul Healing, you will discover how to:

- Super charge your body
- Control pain to feel better
- Reduce stress in your life
- Eliminate negative thoughts
- Eliminate any bad habits
- Achieve your goals with ease
- Turn on your natural healing system to heal health problems.

All you must do is follow the simple techniques for 21 days that is laid out for you in this book.

Let's face it. You deserve to be healthy, successful, and happy. It's your birthright!

INTRODUCTION

15 years of research and study, and the answer was always there…

I didn't know it at the time, but at the age of nine while visiting a friend, I was given the key to healing, and that would change my life forever, and I know it can change your life too!

Like most baby boomers, my parents came from the old country with nothing but memories of hunger, war, and death. My father suffered 6 heart attacks and had the highest blood pressure ever recorded. My mother had cancer. For years they did everything possible to stay healthy. They visited specialist after specialist. They tried every known remedy to them. They even tried some new promising new drugs, but the side effects were so horrible that they had to stop. My mother even drank Naphtha, to try and cure her cancer. I never really knew how much my parents had suffered. They kept working until they died. My mother at age 67 and my father, 2 years later at age 73.

However, the day I received the key to healing, I had no idea how my life was going to change. After years of growing and experiencing life, it became clear to me all at once, there it was – the actual solution for healing disease.

After 15 years of searching, studying, hoping and following advice from teachers of the healing arts, health gurus, reading book after book on every healing modality that I could find, I finally understood the key to healing that was given to me at age nine. I started to apply this key with my clients in my private hypnosis practice. I soon discovered that this key is the one God given ability that we all must use to help the body, mind and soul heal.

That key was in fact, the ability to communicate with the subconscious mind through hypnosis.

PART 2

THE MIND BODY CONNECTION

The connection between the mind and body is not a new discovery. To quote Dr. Hamer: "Through the millennia, humanity has more or less have known that all diseases ultimately have a psychic origin and it became a scientific asset firmly anchored in the inheritance of universal knowledge; it is only modern medicine that has turned our animated

beginnings into a bag full of chemical formulas"

After extensive research of thousands of patients, Dr. Hamer was finally able to conclude that disease is only brought about by a shock (stress) for which we are totally unprepared.

If we can in any way be prepared for the shock event, we will not become ill.

Dr. Lipton's research in cell biology and quantum psychics proves that our bodies can change with simple thinking.

Is it possible to use the mind to heal body illness? Is there really a "mind/body connection" whereby our thoughts and emotions can facilitate healing? YES!

Modern medicine is taking notice of an old notion: Healing involves tending to a person's emotional and spiritual needs as well as the physical. We are embracing the notion of mind-body medicine in increasing numbers, as part of a trend toward the use of complementary and alternative medicine therapies.

Mind-body techniques use the power of the mind to affect body functions. It is understood that the subconscious part of the brain controls all body functions. Nothing happens to your body without a thought. That thought comes from you.

The immune system then, is controlled by the brain, either indirectly through hormones in the bloodstream, or directly through the nerves and neurochemicals.

There is now experimental evidence that "passive emotions", such a grief, feeling of failure, and suppression of anger, produce oversecretion of hormones, which suppress the immune system. We don't yet understand all the ways in which brain chemicals are related to emotions and thoughts, but the important point is that our state of mind has an immediate and direct effect on our state of body. We can change the body by dealing with how we think and feel.

There are two ways in which we can get our bodies and minds to communicate with each other – through emotion and imagery. Emotion and words allow the body to know what is expected of it, and by vividly imagining certain changes we can help the body produce the results.

Hypnosis, however, has a unique advantage over other mind/body techniques above and beyond its capacity to elicit emotions and make imagery more vivid and powerful. It is the capacity for "direct Suggestion". Properly worded direct suggestion to the subconscious mind enables it to actually order the body's immune system to fight and destroy invading cells, viruses, tumors, bacteria and so forth and start repairing diseased or injured tissue, organs, nerves, bones etc. This is a very powerful and important advantage.

Our mental attitude is a powerful influence on our physical health. Attitudes and emotions can either act as a mighty shield and heal us from illness of all kinds - from headaches to cancer or, conversely, can bring on all manners of pains, aches, illness, and disease.

A BRIEF HISTORY

The earliest record of what we now call hypnosis is from the Egyptian culture more that six thousand years ago. The hieroglyphic records in the British Museum appeared with a high priest, illustrated by the markings in his garments, with fingers extended and magnetic rays moving out toward the person in front of him standing with their eyes closed and dead down.

There were special buildings termed "sleep temples" and those who went into the temples were cast into a state in which they remained for as long as seven to ten days while the priest whispered suggestions in their ears.

These were not called suggestion they were called prayer. If the prayer was answered, it meant that the gods had responded, however, if the prayer did not generate a response, they were told that the gods decided they were unworthy or perhaps they should pray to the cat god instead of the frog god.

There is no further written record of hypnosis from that ancient time, and it remained a hidden religious secret, until about 1750. A young man who started out to become a monk learned the art from two Jesuit monks, Father Maximilian Hell, and Father Victor Gassner. He later decided he would not become a monk but would become a physician instead; his name was Frederick Anton Mesmer (a doctor of Vienna).

We are all indebted to Dr. Mesmer because for the first time, what had been a hidden religious secret became exposed to the light of scientific and medical research. Physicians and scientists from all over Europe came to Mesmer's clinic to study the strange occurrences that were part of the daily routine of curing patients. Unfortunately, due to Mesmer's only partial success in curing the blindness of an 18-year-old musician, Maria Theresia Paradis, Mesmer was temporarily discredited, but the interest that he stimulated remained.

The name that emerged from that period of interest and research was "animal magnetism". Mesmer's theory was that planets emit magnetic rays, which we know today as cosmic radiation. This was an amazing discovery because he observed that the moon was the planet closest to the earth and had a powerful effect upon animal life on this planet. He also observed that the phases of the moon affect the oceanic tides and currents and the tides and currents of human emotions.

Mesmer believed that people develop various ailments because the blood and other fluids of the body were lacking in magnetism. His remedy was the use of "lodestones'" the name for natural magnets which he believed to be pieces of the moon that had fallen to earth. By applying these to the body, the magnetic energy would be infused into the bloodstream and the sickness would be cured. That was a mistaken theory, but amazing cures did occur in Mesmer's clinic because of mental expectancy and group suggestion. During the next hundred years, there were many medical researchers' conducting similar investigations of Mesmer's theories.

In 1841, an English physician, Dr. James Braid coined the term "neuro-hypnosis".

Neuro means nerves; *hypnosis* comes form the Greek work “hypnos” which means “sleep”.

What Dr. Braid meant to convey by this term was that hypnosis was a “sleep of the nervous system”. He observed that whenever a person entered this state they relaxed to a degree and in a manner that just didn’t seem possible in any other way. In the years since then, the first part of that name was dropped away, and we were left with the word hypnosis and its mistaken identity with sleep.

For the Egyptians, it was a religious practice and the energy was invested “out there” with the gods or “transcendental” energy. Even with Mesmer, the energy was still ‘out there” in the moon which radiated energy to us. When Braid developed the theory of suggestion, he brought to our awareness the realization that the energy is an internal energy! Since it’s an internal energy, we may have the capacity to direct it, for our own behalf.

We are no longer dependent on the effects of the planets, but we can learn to control and direct this energy within us.

HYPNOSIS; FACT OR FICTION

The Sleeping Prophet, Edgar Cayce would command himself to engage in out-of-body experiences and near-death experiences through self-hypnosis. Under a trance state, he would give psychic reading and diagnoses to people he has never met. His followers documented almost 14,000 journeys unto the spirit realm, made through his subconscious mind or what Cayce referred to as the spirit.

Hypnosis may be one of the most misunderstood and highly underestimated topics and thus controversial to us. Before I delve further in our understanding of the mind body connection, let's review some of the most popular — myths of hypnosis.

When in hypnosis, it may look like your asleep, but you're not. You are fully awake and aware of everything that is going on around you. You are not unconscious. You are just in a very relaxed state. You are not gullible. If you do not wish to accept the suggestion given by the hypnotist, then you will not accept it. You are not weak-minded. In fact, the better your imagination or a higher intelligence, the better your experience will be. You are never out of control. You are always in full control. You will never be out of self-control. You will display the ultimate in mind control.

Now, as for myself, no, I don't have supernatural powers. I'm not casting a Voodoo spell over you. I'm not an apostle of the devil. Neither am I a saint. I'm just your friendly neighbourhood hypnotist.

Some people say, "hypnosis sounds wonderful, but I don't think I can be hypnotized!" Well you may be surprised to learn that you already experience hypnosis daily. Let's look at examples of daily hypnosis.

Watching a movie and becoming trans fixed in the plot.

Immersed in a book and been so transfixed that you did not hear someone come in and speak with you.

Driving home from work and not knowing how you got there.

Working on your computer and hours pass but felt that is was just minutes.

Hypnosis is not witchcraft, mind control, religion, or magic. It is simply a tool that will allow you to tap into the power of your subconscious mind. There are only two reasons when you will not be able to experience hypnosis.

1 - You do not want to be hypnotized.

2 - You have an IQ of less than 70.

Anyone with medical conditions such as epilepsy or mental disabilities should not be hypnotized. Never substitute hypnosis for medical or psychological treatment.

Some people erroneously believe that to be hypnotized you must be weak-minded. In fact, the better your imagination, concentration, and IQ, the better you are as a hypnotic subject. Often if people are having trouble experiencing hypnosis it is because they are trying too hard. Hypnosis happens when you just let go and relax. When in hypnosis, you will ask yourself, "Am I hypnotized?"

It was widely believed that the hypnotist could turn people into zombie-like robotic creatures that obey every command. Sorry to disappoint. When in hypnosis your sense of right and wrong will remain intact. The hypnotist cannot make you do anything that you would not do in a normal state of mind.

On the other side of the spectrum, while some people perceive hypnosis as evil and manipulative, some have prescribed it as a cure-all for all kinds of conditions – from weight loss to finding the "key" to financial success. In fact, specific behavioural changes are the most common use of hypnosis.

Most people try to make behavioural changes based on self-discipline and will power. The problem here is that these are short-term solutions which are inefficient and ineffective to facilitate permanent change. Hypnosis has been proven to be an effective solution.

Results of a comparative study by the American Health Magazine showed that Psychoanalysis had a 38% recovery after 600 sessions. Behavioural therapy had a 72% recovery after 22 sessions, and hypnosis had a 93% recovery after only 6 sessions. In my own practice, I have a 98% recovery in only 3 sessions.

Whatever your goals are, hypnosis can help you achieve them more easily and more quickly. Many people don't realize the awesome power of the subconscious mind has over their lives. The cause of so many "bad habits" are rooted in memories or perceptions that may be forgotten by the conscious mind but retained in the subconscious. Hypnosis helps to access the subconscious mind and affect the desired changes easier and quicker

Although hypnosis is not a panacea, there are many areas where it has proven to be tremendously helpful.

Sounds outstanding but is hypnotism really that effective?

"What the mind causes, the mind can cure". Wellness begins in the mind! Every problem has a cause, and when you eliminate the cause from the computer we call the subconscious mind, the problem disappears. Even Sigmund Freud said "the only way to solve a problem was through the subconscious mind. And the only way to reach the subconscious mind is with hypnosis."

Yes, hypnotism has been utilized as part of the treatment and therapy of various physical and psychological conditions. Through its ability to tap into the subconscious and to intensify focus and concentration, hypnosis can help you be more attuned with your intellectual and emotional capacity; thus helping you modify your habits and behaviors, or wield more control over the way you think and analyze.

PART 3

CHAPTER 1

STRESSED OUT? JUST RELAX

John used to drink two glasses of scotch before dinner every night just to relax enough to make the transition from work to home life. He desperately needed to unwind after a stressful workday as a management executive and was looking for an alternative to drinking when he stumbled upon hypnosis. Now after work John takes a twenty minute "relaxation break" by closing himself off in his bedroom, turning off the lights and the phone and putting on his audio CD. (The same audio CD that is available from me. See page 90 to receive it.) As the guided meditation and music plays, his nerves and his thoughts turn to a "safe place" a mental haven where he goes to escape from the stresses of the outer world. Wherever John is, John knows he is safe, comfortable, and in complete control: no one asking anything of him or wanting anything from him. Here he is relaxed, happy, and at peace with himself and everyone around him.

Here in his own imagination, John is in complete control. The relaxed, good-natured John comes out from his room a completely different person from the stressed and sometimes short-tempered man who went in. John's family members, as well as John are grateful that he has discovered hypnosis.

John is just one of a growing number of people who have found that simple relaxation is an effective, non-drug alternative for stress reduction. You could call this relaxation, "Meditation". Hypnosis is just meditation, but with words and meditation is just hypnosis, without words.

Stress is an ever-present part of everyone's lifestyle and the growing evident link between stress and illness. This includes conditions such as hypertension, heart disease, ulcers, immune deficiency diseases and even cancer. Hypnosis provides welcome relief without side effects.

Hypnosis, simply put, is a relaxed and focused state of mind. Anyone can be trained to enter this state of deep relaxation easily and safely in just a few sessions with my assistance. Once you are shown the simple technique of self-hypnosis, you will be able to place yourself into a deep and relaxed state. Unlike alcohol or drugs, hypnosis can be practiced anytime and anywhere. All that is required is an opportunity to relax for a few minutes. One can practice hypnosis while gazing out of an office window or sitting in a quiet corner of the office lunchroom.

By quieting the mind and body, hypnosis sets into motion a chain reaction of physiological responses, such as hormonal and immune system functionality changes. Hypnosis reduces the effects of stress on the body by thwarting the "flight or fight response, lowering heart rate and blood pressure and relaxing muscle tension. These changes, in turn stimulate other positive changes such as lowered production of stress hormones and increase of protective T-cell production by the immune system.

With more studies every day illustrating the effectiveness of hypnosis for stress reduction and its accompanying health benefits, shouldn't you try hypnosis? It's simple, easy, and pleasant. Contrary to popular myth, a hypnotherapist does not "take over" your mind or influence your thoughts except at your request. You are aware at all times of the suggestions that the hypnotherapist offers, and your mind will automatically reject any suggestion that conflict with your values or beliefs. On the other hand, when the hypnotherapist's suggestion leads you to more relaxation, a healthier and more balanced life, why not accept them with an open mind? Working with me, you can tailor suggestions and imageries to your specific needs and desires.

CHAPTER 2

HYPNO SMOKING

The dangers of smoking have been studied and analyzed for years. The detrimental effect of smoking on people's health and their activities is now public knowledge, and many people who have become addicted to this habit are now looking for ways to quit.

Most stop-smoking programs work at increasing the individual's strength to resist the desire to smoke. They rely on willpower, and for most people that is the worst method for quitting smoking. Will power is rooted in the conscious mind, but smoking is a subconscious activity. Willpower fluctuates like moods and emotions. One day it may be strong the next day it may be weak. How many times have smokers made the New Year's resolution to stop smoking and a few days later find themselves starting up again?

Hypnosis works at eliminating the desire to smoke, whether it's from identification or replacement, the two principle reasons for smoking.

Identification is when the smoker indulges in the habit because the client admires (or associates) with others who smoke, i.e. parents, peers, or celebrities. Identification smoking is the most common and the easiest to eliminate.

Replacement is when smoking takes the place of a previous habit (such as overeating), something that is missing, (such as companionship, love, acceptance, self-esteem, security, independence), or when it fills a void created by anxiety or boredom. For both types of smokers, smoking is both a physical and mental process. So, to be effective, the HypNO smoking program addresses both aspects.

To address the psychological aspect of smoking, I may include an evaluation of why the client started smoking. "What purpose does it serve in their life?" For the replacement smoker a more detailed analysis of their motivation is required. To address the physical aspect of smoking, I may include suggestions that change the perception of the taste from pleasant to unpleasant.

Hypnosis takes advantage of the mind's natural ability to imagine and visualize. The clients picture themselves free from the habit, filled with new health, energy, and vitality. They can see themselves as looking healthier, more attractive, and being more active.

CHAPTER 3

HYPNO DIET WEIGHT LOSS

Many people become overweight when they begin to use food to satisfy an emotional need; to compensate for something they feel is missing in their lives. Some people overeat to compensate for an unpleasant experience. Others eat to reward themselves, or possibly for entertainment. Food can be used to compensate for a lack of love, to offset fear, to overcome frustration, to deal with boredom, or sometimes even to avoid sex.

For those people, dieting alone will not be enough to lose the weight and keep it off. Dieting never eliminates the subconscious need for excess food. It's just a form of self-torture one endures: Counting on a roller coaster ride of weight gain & loss, never letting go of the desire for excess food until one eventually gives in to subconscious desires.

A hypnosis session with me will do more than just modify an individual's behaviour. It addresses all issues that may be affecting their eating habits. I will ask; "When do you overeat?" "Where do you overeat?" and most importantly, "why?". I will also examine the client's self-esteem and self-confidence. Do these areas of self-image require strengthening? The hypnosis session will help the client look back on their life and locate the event (or events) that led to the current attitude toward food. This is the first step in eliminating the subconscious desire for excessive eating.

In the session, I will instill a new attitude toward eating, such as "I am satisfied with small amounts of healthy food". As a bonus to the session, I include an audio CD to reinforce the new attitude. When used for 21 days, the attitude becomes a permanent part of the client's outlook on life. New eating habits are formed that will last a lifetime. The weight easily stays off, and the rollercoaster ride is over.

CHAPTER 4

ARE YOU IN PAIN?

We all suffer pain at one time or another. Migraine headaches, back pain, chronic pain from illness or injury, birthing pains, pain from surgery or other medical procedures. Whenever we're in pain, we want immediate relief. So, we call the doctor for medication. We take it and most of the time it helps. But other times it doesn't help… enough… or for long enough. And sometimes we prefer not to take strong medications of fear of addiction.

Is there an alternative? Is there a safe way to be pain free without medication?

Hypnosis, in addition to regular medical treatment, has several advantages in pain management. First, it doesn't require drugs. In fact, studies show that patients with chronic diseases who practice hypnosis requires fewer analgesics to maintain pain relief. They also suffer less anxiety about their pain and greater comfort during medical procedures. Hypnosis returns a sense of control to the patient and it doesn't have any side effects.

Study after study have proven hypnotherapy to be the *preferred* treatment for reducing migraines.

With such impressive results, why do we reach for a pill bottle instead of the natural relaxing, healing capacities within our own minds? The answer is obvious. Most of us don't know how to practice self-hypnosis. Many of us are not aware of its success rate. Still others hold outdated fearful notions that hypnosis involves "mind control", that hypnosis is the work of the devil.

That's unfortunate because hypnosis or "hypnotherapy" also commonly referred to because of its therapeutic appreciation is a resource that should be explored by all who suffer pain. It provides continual pain management that, once established, can be monitored, and adjusted by the client. It returns a sense of control back to the client without side effects except an overall increased feeling of wellbeing and relaxation.

CHAPTER 5

OPERATING ROOM CHATTER

Can any comments made during surgery by your doctors, nurses and other staff affect the outcome of your operation? Can you hear their conversations even while you're anaesthetized? The answer to both questions is an emphatic "YES".

The anaesthetized state simulates a deep state of hypnosis rather than "being totally out" state we normally think of with total unconsciousness. Being unconscious means that the conscious part of the brain is not functioning, but the subconscious is always awake. Because of this, comments made about the patient during surgery can have a profound effect on the outcome of the surgery.

The last thing a patient should hear, even in a stupor, is "this looks bad" or "he may not make it". Operating room staff should always speak positively during the surgery as if the patient is awake. Such suggestions could be as simple as "you are doing very well; looks great;" or they could be more elaborate and specific to the surgery, such as when the doctor introduces the new organ, the doctor could say "The organ will be easily accepted by your body and will function perfectly."

This is reason enough to ask your doctor and his staff to monitor their operating room chatter. Nonetheless, you can still reap the benefits of positive reinforcement made during surgery by having me supply you with an audio CD for pre- and post-surgery. Check with your doctor before showing up in the operating room with your CD, but since more and more patients are listening to CD's during surgery, the doctor should not be surprised at your request.

An even better idea would be to visit me one or more times prior to the surgery to pre-program the mental suggestions for positive results even more strongly. Armed with knowledge and a positive attitude, you will be ready for a successful operation and speedy recovery.

CHAPTER 6

STROKE RECOVERY WITH HYPNOSIS

As we age, we become more vulnerable to disease processes such as high blood pressure, heart disease and stroke, but an interesting case study by two Los Angeles researchers shed doubt on traditional views about the chances for recovery from at least one of these dreaded diseases – Stroke.

Widely accepted medical viewpoints claim that all recovery from a Stroke will stop at about six months after occurrence of the vascular accident. By using hypnosis, a technique not normally associated with the treatment of stroke in hospitals, researchers helped a 66-

year-old woman regain several physical capacities, including limited use of a disabled arm and the ability to walk without a cane.

Under hypnosis, the patient was guided through imagery that recalled memories of previous abilities, including swimming in a river as a child. In addition to the hypnosis sessions, the woman was trained in self-hypnosis to help reinforce what she had learned to practice at home.

One-year post-stroke follow-up showed verifiable improvement in the physical capabilities of the patient. As an interesting note, the hypnotherapy was instituted at the request of the patient, after a neurologist had concluded that she would not likely gain any further improvement in her physical condition. Sometimes, it seems, the patient knows best.

Imagery works on the mind in a way that is not yet clearly understood, but I believe that the subconscious mind does not know the difference between seeing something that is real or imagined. The subconscious minds responsibility is to act out any programming that it receives. So, if the mind can conceive it, the body will achieve it.

CHAPTER 7

REGRESSION THERAPY

Age regression is one of the most powerful tools available to me as a hypnotist. With it, I can guide the person back in time and help them examine the event(s) that initially triggered the problem from an objective point of view. Once the subconscious reveals the cause, the problem can be eliminated.

A good example is the case of "Cathy". She came to see me to discuss a personal development that she did not understand. As far back as she could remember, she had always felt sadness when visitors left her home: a situation which become increasingly troublesome. The emotional upsets were no longer limited to loves ones but happened whenever anyone went out the door. The feelings grew stronger, which resulted in tears and severe crying spells bordering on hysteria.

After interviewing her, I concluded that some event in her childhood had resulted in a psychological imprint that had either been forgotten or had not been consciously recognized as the cause. (Up to 90% or even more of our problems that we have as adults, started in our childhood.)

She was hypnotized, and the subconscious took her back to the time and place the problem occurred. Cathy explained that she was three years old, sitting on the stairs in her home, looking down into the living room. Her father had just died and was lying in the living room. She was called down and told to kiss her father good-bye, which she did.

The well-meaning family wanted to avoid a situation where a child, not understanding what death was, would not constantly be expecting her father to return. They explained that when her father would be taken out through "the door", he would be gone forever and would never return.

Without realizing what they have done, they had created an association between death and doors that remained locked in her subconscious. To her three-year-old mind, there was no understanding, only an authoritative statement that going out the door would lead to something terrible. (She was unknowingly hypnotized).

Once the subconscious realized the incorrect connection that was made with death and doors, the subconscious immediately corrected the issue was removed.

If Cathy had gone for traditional psychoanalysis, it might have required months if not years to discover the cause of the problem, but I was able to help her in just two sessions.

CHAPTER 8

EASY ELIMINATION OF FEARS AND PHOBIA

One of the most common reasons people visit me is to overcome a fear or phobia. Most fears develop during childhood but can also develop during adulthood.

Fears are a natural part of life. Everyone fears something such as being robbed or being hurt in an accident. This type of fear is not necessarily bad as it may prompt you to take precautions, such as locking doors or wearing safety belts.

Many fears are the results of repressed memories. One indication of whether a fear is physical or psychological is the duration of the reaction.

Psychological reactions are usually triggered by anticipation and become less intense once the anticipated event begins. Physical reactions tend to become more intense once the event begins.

If one feels intense fear frequently, they may begin to lose control. They can become afraid to feel the fear; and go out of their way to avoid anything that might trigger it. When this happens, the fear has become a phobia. (A fear may also be considered a phobia when an individual can feel the sensation of being afraid without recognizing what triggered the feeling.)

When a fear or phobia is limiting, interfering with your lifestyle, or causing you to avoid something you would like to do, then it should be treated.

More severe cases are often the result of traumatic childhood event. Most of the time the event can no longer be recalled by the conscious mind but is still retained in the subconscious. Every event that has ever happens to us, from the day we are born to the day of our death is remembered. Every touch, every smell, everything that we hear and see, good or bad is stored to our subconscious mind.

In mild cases, where a person recognizes the cause of the fear and would like to control their reaction, I would use post hypnotic suggestions that would help with their breathing, slow their heart, and bring them to a controlled and relaxed state of mind. This allows them to deal with the fear in a calm and rational manner.

In more severe cases I will employ age regression and correct the Phobia that way.

CHAPTER 9

ACHIEVE YOUR GOALS

Everyone has dreams. Some dream of love; some dream of wealth; some dream of success. But very few learn how to turn dreams into reality. One of the reasons for this is something that has recently been identified as the "Playpen Syndrome". The playpen syndrome describes a bureaucracy. People and agencies that want to avoid being bothered by ambition, creativity, new thinking, or progress propagates it. It stifles individuality and prevents the achievement of goals.

The Playpen Syndrome begins when children learn from parents, teachers, or other authority figures that they will only be liked if they do as they are told; if they create problems, they won't be liked. Authoritative figures don't intentionally create this attitude. The young impressionable mind develop the idea that they will be liked if they don't cause any problems.

This, unfortunately, stifles creativity and sends a message to the subconscious mind that maintaining the status quo is the same as being liked. This become a goal in their lives. They do not learn to explore, take risks, or seek solutions to everyday problems or challenges. Children today are being rewarded for just taking part. Winning or losing is no longer part of the game any longer.

Without any real motivation to improve their skills and set goals due to the Playpen Syndrome young adults begin working in an environment that that gives them job security with benefits, regardless of their skill level or the quality of their work. Their lives are managed for by someone else, so they never take the initiative to take control of their lives to make their dreams come true.

Motivation and attitude are just as essential as proper goal setting. You must have a strong desire to achieve your goals. You must have confidence to know that you can succeed. With hypnosis I can find these things that are there within you and bring them out to strengthen your belief and confidence. You can achieve your dreams.

CHAPTER 10

LEARNING AND MEMORY

Learning should be a lifelong process for everyone. The potential rewards of continuously learning new things cannot be overstated. Whether learning new skills for a job, or studying a topic of personal interest, everyone can benefit from continuing education.

There are many factors that may impede the learning process. The two most important factors are low self-esteem and lack of motivation. Poor study habits, poor memory, lack of reward, poor nutrition, and even medication can also adversely affect an individual's ability to learn new things. With hypnosis I can definitely help.

Motivation is emotional and comes from within. Knowing the benefits of success is not enough. Feeling a strong desire to acquire those benefits is essential. If too many of these desires compete for the individual's time and attention, he/she may not be able to focus. Desires can lose their strength so less will be accomplished. The individual should set priorities. Once that is accomplished, hypnosis can reinforce those priorities and strengthen their focus.

Self-esteem is built up with a series of successes and rewards. Setting interim goals as steps can help to achieve them. Each time a goal is achieved, the individual should recognize their success and reward themselves.

But for most people hypnosis can provide insight, guidance, and direction to establish personal learning goals, boost self-esteem, create motivation and improved memory.

CHAPTER 11

TEST TAKING JITTERS

The decision to turn a life-long interest into a career in massage therapy seemed only natural to Bob. Bob had always worked well with his hands and all his friends said that he gave the best back rubs; However, once he was enrolled in massage therapy school, Bob's dream became a nightmare. As his courses progressed, Bob discovered that the large amount of memorization required to pass the tests became increasingly challenging for him. He saw his dream slipping away as he fought harder to memorize the material while his grades, increasingly dropped. He knew he had to do something fast.

Bob's friend, also a massage therapist, suggested that bob try hypnosis for test taking anxiety. Bob agreed to give it a try.

Bob didn't know what to expect during his first visit with me, so I quickly put him at ease and explained the process of hypnosis and how it worked. I answered all his questions and put to rest about any misconceptions about hypnosis and any concerns that he had about "losing control." I told him that he would be in full control and that he would not be a mindless zombie under my control as portrayed in the movies. I explained that he would be in a very pleasant state of deep relaxation from which he could come out of at any time. While in this altered state of hypnosis, Bob's subconscious mind would accept suggestions or ideas that he perceived to be useful and beneficial for him to pass his tests.

I asked Bob to mentally visualize himself in his study area, picturing his desk, books, papers, and even any beverages he would normally have on hand to drink. Then I asked Bob to roll play in his mind, his study habits, suggesting that his mind would be relaxed and receptive, and that he would remember fully and easily the information that he read or studied. I further suggested that when questioned about materials he had studied, either verbally or on a test, his mind would instantly recall all information on to a conscious level.

Bob's dream came true. He graduated in the top of his class, thanks to a little help (and some good advice about trying hypnosis) from his friend.

If you or someone you know suffers from test-taking anxiety or trouble with studying and memorization, hypnosis might be the answer.

CHAPTER 12

ATHLETIC PERFORMANCE

Training only the body and ignoring the mind invites a mediocre performance. Hypnosis won't turn the weekend warrior into a national champion, but it can help anyone achieve his or her personal best. How? By arming them with improved concentration, a clear focus on goal achievement, the ability to visualize, and most importantly, a strong positive attitude.

Most sports psychologists will agree: 80% of an athlete's performance is due to attitude and mental conditioning.

Concentration is vital, but sometimes difficult to develop. Hypnosis has been an effective means of improving concentration skills. Post hypnotic suggestions can help the athlete focus on the task at hand and shut out distractions.

Goal setting is also essential. Without a goal in mind, it is pointless to begin any task. A goal must be specific. Otherwise it would be impossible to tell when the goal has been reached. Playing tennis better is to general of a suggested goal, but improving a serve or backhand is easily attainable, and successful attainment is easily recognized.

Visualization can also provide an essential element to achieve success. Mental rehearsal before the performance can lead to increased confidence during the performance.

Many professionals employ some form of self-hypnosis to help them achieve their success. One such well known golfer is Tiger Woods. He started using hypnosis at a very young age. His father employed a sports psychologist that used hypnosis and trained Tiger on how to visualize. He not only visualized the perfect swing, but also learned to control distractions. Tiger performed self-hypnosis on the course as he played. The results speak for themselves.

The most important factor is a positive attitude. Hypnosis can help change negative thoughts and eliminate performance anxiety. The occasional poor performance will not cause irritation, anger, discouragement, or any other detrimental emotional reaction any longer. As a result, concentration, coordination, and technique will all improve, and enjoyment will be greatly enhanced.

CHAPTER 13

RELAXED AND PAINLESS CHILDBIRTH

Hypnosis has been used to control pain during labour and delivery for more than a century, but the introduction of anesthesia during the late 19th century led to the decline of its utilization. It is easier provide drug to a patient than work with her for a few weeks before her giving birth.

Hypnotherapy has been found to be effective in providing pain relief, thus reducing the need for any drugs. Hypnosis has also been helpful in both managing various complications of pregnancy (such as premature labour) and reducing the likelihood of premature labour in high risk patients. It has also been effective in the treatment of hypertension associated with pregnancy and turning of breech babies to the vertex presentation. Hypnosis preparation reduces anxiety, fear, tension, reduces birth complications, and promotes a rapid recovery process. With hypnosis the expectant mother has control which empowers her in managing her pregnancy and birth experience.

The best results with hypnosis occur when the expectant mother is introduced to hypnosis a few weeks before labour begins. This way she can practice the hypnosis skills she will need during her birthing. However, introduction at any time is better than not using hypnosis at all.

Studies have shown that hypnosis helped alleviate pain during childbirth, especially for first time moms. While self-hypnosis gave patients greater control over stress, anxiety and pain of medical operations and childbirth. It was also found to shorten labour.

Another exciting effect with hypnosis has been shown to very effective in turning breach and posterior (sunny side up) babies, in fact more successful than the manual technic.

CHAPTER 14

SPIRIT RELEASE THERAPY

What you are about to read was as amazing to me as its going to be for you. This was my first encounter of a spiritual account or you could call it messaging or contact from the other side.

Over the past year I studied about Spiritualism and how hypnosis could be connected somehow to the spirt world. I had just finished reading a book by William J. Baldwin titled, *Spirit Releasement Therapy.* He stated that one could connect to the spirit world through hypnosis.

Well, In this session, this is exactly what had happened. A young lady came in for a weight loss session. When I had suggested to her, while under hypnosis, that she was here to lose the unwanted weight. She replied "NO!" I was not speaking with the young lady anymore but with an older woman who believed that this young lady was her granddaughter, and she did not want her to lose the weight.

According to contemporary science, spirit attachment and or possession is impossible: outworn concepts of interest to anthropologists and historians. In my practice I have recognized that some of the memories and emotions of the clients are those of someone else, an attached sprit of a deceased human being. This condition has historically been labelled as sprit possession. A more accurate term is sprit attachment. This is a more common event than true spirit possession; lies a complete takeover of the human host. It's believed that between 70 to 90% of the population have experienced an attachment or influence by one or more entities at the same time.

Our language reflects an inner awareness of this condition. How often have you heard these phrases: "What's got into you"? "What possessed me to do that"? "I'm not myself today" "they are a different person". The possibilities of spirit attachment and or complete possession has been recognized or at least theorized in every culture.

An attachment can be benevolent in nature or self-serving to fulfill a personal need of the spirit.

Spirit release therapy is not based on any religious belief system. There isn't any exhortation or prayer, ritual, or superstitious based litany. The approach is clear, rational, methodical, and complete.

In contrast to adversarial confrontation of traditional exorcists, the motivation that I believe, and use is one of compassion for confused and misguided earthbound spirit.

With the use of hypnosis, I establish contact with the spirit. It then becomes necessary to persuade it to leave and go into the LIGHT. As previously stated, this kind of therapy can bring dramatic benefits, it is important to clarify that this is only one aspect of the treatment process. Regression to cause, soul retrieval, forgiveness, and aura healing through lifestyle changes, may also be needed to complete the healing.

At death the spirit usually passes easily in the LIGHT, the white brilliance seen during a near death experience. However, if a spirit is confused, disoriented due to a traumatic death, or has "unfinished business", it may attach itself to relatives, friends, or anyone that it feels a connection to, in this life or a past life. It may not be able to reach the LIGHT and become earthbound. Sometimes the spirit does not realized it has died and thinks it's still alive. It continues to try to live a normal life only to find out that something is wrong when no one pays attention to them as they've become a spirit. It's at this point that the spirit attaches to someone trying to find its way.

Vulnerability to spirit attachment varies due to predisposition, health, and circumstances. Negativity, pain, anger, illness, surgery, injury, addictions, and organ transplants recipients all are good attractors for a spirit attachment due to the lack of protective energy in our body (our Aura).

Certain individuals seem to attract sprits more often than others. Frequently spirits are attracted to those who had similar problems as they did in life and in some cases, attachment may be purely accidental.

The signs and symptoms of attachment vary, greatly. The most common are unexplained fatigue, unexplained depression, sudden changes in mood, hearing a voice, addictions of all kinds, changes in personality or behaviour, confusion, anomalous sexual behaviour as unexplained somatic symptoms. The effect of spirit attachment may be so slight as to be imperceptible or so great as to cause incapacity. It is important to realize that there may be other causes for the above symptoms.

With the use of hypnosis, I establish contact with the earthbound spirit. It then becomes necessary to persuade it to leave and go into the LIGHT. As previously stated, spirit releasement can bring dramatic benefits, but it is only one aspect of the treatment process. Regression to cause, soul retrieval, forgiveness, and aura healing through lifestyle changes, may also be needed to complete the healing.

Spirit releasement therapy offers quick and effective treatment, without subjecting clients to the lengthy, unpleasant, and sometimes harmful effects of medication and other psychological treatment. It is true to say that modern psychology does not recognize the existence of the soul. In not recognizing the soul there is no possibility of being shown a map, which includes the entire nature of the human experience, the wholeness of being.

CHAPTER 15

LIFE-AFTER-DEATH YOUR REAL LIFE

Life-After-Death Real-Life (LADRL) hypnosis is both an extension and evolution beyond Past Life Regression. This is because the technique of Life-After-Death experience allows access to our soul in a higher state of consciousness we call the super conscious or ultra-mind. This procedure, also called spiritual hypnosis. This permits subjects to connect with their soul-self. Thus, clients can bridge their physical body and connect with a more permanent immortal life in the spirit world.

Once removed from the physical world to one's "eternal self" a client can see their entire evolutionary karmic growth pattern over a vast amount of earth time in many bodies. One learns why those bodies were chosen; the "fit" between the experiences encountered in past and present lives and the lessons they bring. When you are in the state of super consciousness, you can transcend identification with physical incarnations to access a deeper, eternal nature that actively records the lessons of those lives as part of an evolutionary growth of soul consciousness. Past and present human live are but alter-egos of an eternal identity. In this state of heightened perception and understanding, clients are then able to find their own answers to the age-old questions such as: "Who am I?" "Why am I here?" "Where do I come from?"

One of the most profound spiritual experiences available to individuals who undergo Life-After-Death Real-life (LADRL) session are in direct contact with personal teachers known as spirit guides. These wise beings have been assigned to us since our creation and directly connect with clients during their sessions in such a meaningful way that the encounter becomes "therapeutic". This knowledge in a conscious state promotes a transcendental awareness of having a personal relationship with a higher power.

What A Life-After-Death Real-Life Session Offers You

Over the years many methods to promote access to higher spiritual states of consciousness have been developed and described. Meditation practices have been pursued for millennia, but now Out-of-Body techniques and hypnosis are actively researched, popularized in books, and practiced by many. These powerful methods are becoming widely available is due to the understanding that we have reached the age of Aquarius in the year 2012. This is the only real way to understand the world we live in. It appears that at this juncture in the history of humanity that there is a need for transcendental spiritual experiences to be made available to more than, a disciplined few. These are difficult times from both a social and spiritual perspective.

Life-After-Death Real Life (LADRL) is a means to consciously experience our own permanent identity and the realm in which our soul resides, while answering the fundamental questions… "Who Am I?" and "Why Am I Here Now?" This procedure requires entry into very deep Hypnosis. We use the subconscious mind in this way because the subconscious is the seeing eye to the spiritual world.

You may know this as the "third eye". LADRL assists individuals

to realize themselves as spiritual beings… not through belief, but through an actual conscious experience of that heritage. As a result of a deepened perception of one's own immortal soul, values and the priorities in one's lifetime, emotions, and actions that spring from them – change. For this reason, before being guided in LADRL session, it is highly recommended that prospective clients first experience a Past Life Regression.

PART 4

CHAPTER 16

WORDS OF CAUTION

Hypnotism is a neutral force – it is neither good nor bad. Its value depends on who wields it, and how it will be used. Mind control, the power of suggestion, and tapping into the subconscious, can be dangerous if abused.

Hypnotism is more vulnerable to abuse because it does not take great effort for someone to be able to learn how to do it. Anybody can practice it and achieve a minimum of success. And although the effect may be temporary or minimal, hypnotism has the capacity to alter something in the way the subject may think, behave, or decide in the future.

Historian David Lewis revealed that Adolf Hitler was once hypnotized, and this may have been the root of the kind of life he practiced. Lewis claimed that in 1918, Hitler believed he had gone completely blind despite many diagnoses from doctors that nothing was wrong with his eyes. Through hypnosis, a doctor suggested to Hitler that indeed, he has lost his eyesight but through willpower he could make himself see again "That's because God made him an exceptional person". The hypnosis influenced Hitler so much that he embraced life believing he was exceptional, and the rest, as they say is history.

Thus, only a qualified medical doctor should attempt to diagnose a person and analyze what affects them and then prescribe an appropriate treatment.

It is always best to seek professional medical advice first when you are experiencing pain or illness. Not doing so could lead to life-threatening consequences. Just imagine if I hypnotized the pain away of someone who has a serious disease. If that person I hypnotized did not experience the discomfort brought about by the illness, they would not go to the doctor for a check-up. This could lead to dangerous outcomes and might negatively affect the health and life of the person.

CHAPTER 17

HOW IT FEELS TO BE HYPNOTIZED

Close your eyes for ten seconds. That's what hypnosis feel's like. There's nothing to feel except a sense of relaxation.

It can be hard to allow yourself to relax if you think that you surrender all control of your behaviours to me while under hypnosis. In hypnosis you can hear, smell, feel, taste, and see everything that is going on around you. The hypnotic state is exactly like when you get into bed, close your eyes and you are waiting to fall asleep.

In fact, when you are in hypnosis, you are in more control than when you are in the normal daily state. While your body is relaxed, your subconscious mind will be fully alert and aware of the suggestions it is receiving. You may even find that your mind begins to wander, and you may ask yourself if you're hypnotized.

You may feel tingling or warmth throughout your body. That's good, as this is an indication of deep hypnosis. You may even have a distorted sense of time. You may feel like you have been in hypnosis for just a few minutes, but it's been sixty minutes or more.

CHAPTER 18

WHERE & WHEN SHOULD I DO SELF HYPNOSIS?

I would recommend that you experience your self-hypnosis session at home. Make sure your spot is relaxing and conducive to your activity. Dim the lights. Adjust the room temperature according to your preference. Sit or recline in a comfortable chair or lie on your bed. Turn your phone off.

Many of my clients use hypnosis during their normal day activities such as when they are on a break at work, on a bus or train. IF you're living with other people, pick a scheduled time where there will be fewer distractions: your housemates may be away at work or at school, or by the time everybody's asleep. If you're living alone, do it when you least expect people to drop by, call, or send you texts. Better yet, put your phone on "in a meeting mode".

I would recommend that you experience your hypnotic session reclined in a chair or lying in your bed and let your significant other or kids know you are not to be disturbed unless an emergency occurs.

Find a quiet spot, away from the hustle and bustle of the house. Make sure your spot is relaxing and conducive to relaxation. Surround yourself with pillows and cushions. Make sure you feel as comfortable as possible.

CHAPTER 19

SELF-HYPNOSIS SESSION

Below is your self-hypnosis script. This script will allow you to tap into the power of your mind and to reach your desired outcome by programming your subconscious. For the best results, you have my permission to record the following self-hypnosis script onto an audio CD or your phone and play it to yourself. Record the following script in a slow, calm, relaxing voice.

"I am now going to hypnotize myself for the purpose of relaxing my body and taking away all tension. I now can feel myself relaxing and sinking into the chair or bed and every muscle of my body is now relaxed and at rest. Everything now feels very, very comfortable. I now feel so good to just relax and let everything go. With every breath that I take, I become more and more relaxed. My body now seems so worm, comfortable and relaxed . . . and as the pleasant warmth of relaxation begins to penetrate through every muscle of my being, I am relaxing even more in my chair or bed. Everything is very pleasant, safe, comfortable, and relaxing.
My eyes are beginning to become very, very, heavy, and very, very tired. It is now so hard to keep my eyelids open. They are so heavy and so tired . . .but they won't close yet because I am concentrating on becoming more and more relaxed".

Repeat the above script 3 times.
See page 90 for an advanced technique.

This second part of the script is the programming section. This section is where you add your own suggestion (goal).

My eyelids are now beginning to close. My eyelids are closing, down, down, down. One ... two . . . closing down ... three, very heavy and so tired . . . four. . . five, closing down, six . . . seven, closing "Now as I count slowly from one to ten, my eyes are closing down, heavy eyelids . . . eight . . . nine closing tightly . . . ten, eyes closed.

I am relaxed. . . my head is dropping forward into my chest feeling very relaxed. I am now very relaxed calm and safe. I now feel myself sinking, sinking down, and becoming very relaxed and calm. My body is perfectly relaxed, and my mind is free of all concerns and worries. With every breath that I take, the deeper I go, and the deeper I go, the better I feel." I AM ... (add your goal here and repeat the goal 10 times)

Having reached this point, you may think to yourself that nothing is happening. **Not true.** Your mind is now open to suggestions that can change your life.

Important note. Only do one suggestion (goal) at a time, and for it to take hold, you must do this at least for 21 days. Try and do this at the same time every day.

Repeat your positive suggestion to yourself at least ten time when in the state of hypnosis. You may find yourself dozing gently off to sleep. That's okay, you will awaken shortly. If you have repeated to yourself your suggestion ten times, then it's time to come out of hypnosis. Tell yourself that it's time to emerge from hypnosis. Start to count from one to five and with each count tell yourself that you are feeling better and that all feeling to your body is returning. Once you reach the count of five, open your eyes and take a nice deep breath.

Use this simple technique for the next 21 days and you will see changes in your life. You'll be surprised at how powerful it can be.

CHAPTER 20

CORRECT HYPNOTIC SUGGESTIONS

Prior to your self-hypnosis session you will want to form correct hypnotic suggestions. Your suggestions should always be phrased in the positive, never in the negative. You would also phrase them in the present.

Here is a weight loss example suggestion:

Correct Example:
"I now weight 78 kilograms and find greater satisfaction with smaller, healthier portions of food."

Incorrect Example:
"I'm on my way to losing weight and stop eating foods that are bad for me."

In the incorrect example, you will notice it is phrased in the negative, giving up foods and losing weight. In addition, you will notice the incorrect phrasing of timing. Your subconscious mind will hear these suggestions and take them literally. It will think <u>you are on your way,</u> but it's not time <u>yet</u> to lose the weight.

Think about those area of your life you would like to improve and then work on one specific area during your self-hypnosis session. Don't work on multiple goals in the same session. Think of one specific goal you would like to achieve. Record that goal in the script. Then start to structure suggestions that will allow you to achieve it. Be positive, be in the present and be brief.

Edit your suggestions down to simple sentences. In a typical hypnotic session, you should not use no more than four suggestions that support the single goal you have chosen.

Here is a Stress Control Suggestion:

Correct Example:
"I am now relaxed, and I release stress and those things I cannot control."

Incorrect Example:
"My life will be less stressed when I worry less about those professional and personal worries that are out of my control."

Repetition of each suggestion is important to achieve that desired goal. Repeat each suggestion 10 times per session.

If you find yourself having trouble with the session or even scripting your goal, just contact me and I'll be happy to help you.

If for any reason there's an emergency or your attention is needed during your session, you will immediately emerge yourself to respond appropriately. Emerge means to come to a full alert normal state.

While you are in the state of hypnosis, your subconscious mind will be fully alert and aware of the suggestions it is receiving. You may find your mind begins to wander, that's all right because you are accepting suggestions at the subconscious level and wandering is being done by the conscious mind. All outside stimuli will become irrelevant. Your focus will be directly on the words of suggestions you give yourself and your breathing will be light and rhythmic.

Self-hypnosis can be a relaxing, soothing experience; helping you to loosen up and ease your tensions. It is a form of meditation with words that allows you to converse with yourself. It is a way to de-stress and leave your worries for a while. On a short-term vision, self-hypnosis can help improve your learning threshold, sharpen your memory, and be alert during an exam week or an important presentation at work. It can hold your hand when you're planning to face an emotionally draining situation. It can help you clear the clutter from your mind after a full schedule.

Practiced regularly, it can lead you to more understanding of yourself and others. It may also change the way you lead your life, make decisions, or handle relationships.

The power of self-hypnosis allows you to stop and slow down. Sometimes some very basic things such as these are neglected in our day-to-day routine. Practicing self-hypnosis and just relaxing may sound so simple at first. But once tasked to do it, some of us may find the seemingly simple step of staying put (being still for a while) very difficult. With our multi-tasking, short attention-span culture, staying still and doing nothing seems like a task unto itself. But once you get down to it and do it, the rest will eventually follow.

CHAPTER 21

HOW CAN YOU PROVE TO YOURSELF THAT YOUR HYPNOTIZED?

Here is an advanced, little technique that you can use to validate to yourself that you are in a state of hypnosis. This test should occur after the first script. Give yourself the suggestion that as you relax, your mouth will begin to fill with saliva and as you swallow, it will take you down deeper in to relaxation. When your mouth begins to fill with saliva then you know you are hypnotized, and your subconscious mind is responding to suggestion!

CHAPTER 22

HOW LONG SHOULD YOUR HYPNOSIS SESSION LAST?

There is no set time requirement for a hypnotic session. It only takes a few minutes to enter this state of mind and program oneself for health, wealth, and happiness. The more you practice hypnosis, the easier it will be for you to enter the state. But I must stress to you that you must do the session every day for the 21 days for the subconscious mind to take hold of your goal.

You will notice a distinct change in temperature will occur. As you enter extreme relaxation, your pulse rate begins slowing down, thus triggering a change in body warmth. This will vary from client to client. Most clients will usually feel cold, but once they've entered the state of hypnosis, they don't notice it.

After twenty-one days, you will not consciously notice any programmed changes because the changes have become a subconscious act, which will happen automatically. The only thing you will notice is that you are now healthy, successful, and happy.

PART 5

CHAPTER 23

THE FUTURE OF HYPNOSIS

After two hundred years, we are just beginning to enter a phase where hypnosis will grow exponentially and improve the lives of those who utilize this powerful tool. I believe with the current research in neuroscience, and the realization by both individuals and corporations, hypnosis can be extremely valuable.

Hypnosis has become popular with audiences who enjoy the comedy stage hypnotists and hypnotherapy will continue to grow rapidly over the next several years. The public is starting to explore holistic options to meet their health needs and hypnosis satisfies that requirement. Not only the public, but professional sports teams, and corporation are excited by the opportunities the field offers.

Hypnosis is a wonderful sales tool because it allows one to program themselves to become self-reliant, motivated, and more productive. In addition, I believe as old sales techniques become dated, the new sales professional will learn to rely on ethical rapport building tools instead of the hard sell techniques of the past. My Hypnowords Sales training program is the perfect tool to learn.

The Hypnowords Sales training program is all about building rapport and gaining client's trust. Obviously, I'm not talking about the old, tired, clinches "agree with whatever the customer says and ask about their interests." In the future, the most successful sales professional will be knowledgeable in the latest rapport building techniques and an expert in applying them in any sales call.

CHAPTER 24

CONCLUSION

I have made an earnest endeavour in this book to tell you about hypnosis, what it is, what it is not, what it can do for you, and how to hypnotize yourself. I wish you much success personally and professionally and hope you will use the power of hypnosis to create a more rewarding future for yourself and for your loved ones, and I hope to see you soon at one of my comedy hypnosis shows, seminar or hypnosis workshop or even a private session.

If you feel that you need help, or have any questions or comments, please do not hesitate to contact me.

Alex Szwed CCHt.
Website: www.1hourhypnosis.com

MEET YOUR HYPNOTIST

Alex Szwed, Hypnotherapist, Author,
Grief Recovery Specialist and Spiritual Minister.

Alex is certified by the following organizations:

National Guild of Hypnotists
American Board of Medical Hypnotherapy
Institute of Medical Hypnosis
Breakthrough Institute
Mottin & Johnson Hypnosis Institute
Omni Hypnosis Training Center
Zur Institute
Grief Recovery Institute

ALSO BY ALEX SZWED

Assorted titles of Hypnosis audio CDs

Assorted Whisper affirmation audio CDs

Hypnowords Sales Training

Mega Self-Healing

Wealth Magnet Program

Hypnotist Certification Training

Life-After-Death Real Life

Mini Guide to Ghost Hunting

Please contact me if you're interested or would like more information on any of these titles.

SPECIAL READER BONUS

As an exclusive and special gift for readers of *21 Days To Mind, Body & Soul Healing* I would like to send you a free Deep Relaxation and Stress Reduction audio CD. This is a perfect complement to this book because you will have the opportunity to experience deep relaxation and stress reduction.

www.1hourhypnosis.com

Made in the USA
Monee, IL
23 February 2021

60846881R00056